The Ultimate Self-Teaching Method! Level Two

Play Ukulele Today!

A Complete Guide to the Basics

PLAYBACK+
Speed • Pitch • Balance • Loop

To access audio visit:
www.halleonard.com/mylibrary

6656-2524-0807-6033

by John R. Nicholson

Dedicated to ukulele master John King

Recording Credits:
John R. Nicholson: Ukulele, Vocals & Narration

ISBN 978-1-4234-6601-7

HAL•LEONARD®
CORPORATION

7777 W. BLUEMOUND RD. P.O. BOX 13819 MILWAUKEE, WI 53213

In Australia Contact:
Hal Leonard Australia Pty. Ltd.
4 Lentara Court
Cheltenham, Victoria, 3192 Australia
Email: ausadmin@halleonard.com.au

Visit Hal Leonard Online at
www.halleonard.com

Introduction

Track 1

Welcome to *Play Ukulele Today! Level Two*. This book is a continuation of *Play Ukulele Today! Level One* and is designed to introduce you to tablature, fingerpicking, strumming, and more of everything you need to know to play chords and melodies on your ukulele.

About the Recording

The accompanying audio takes you through each lesson step-by-step, playing each example. The best way to learn the material is to alternate between practicing on your own first and then listening to the audio. With *Play Ukulele Today! Level Two*, you can learn at your own pace. If there is anything that you don't understand the first time through, go back and listen to the teacher's explanation over again. Every musical track has been given its own track number, so if you want to practice a song, you can find it easily.

On musical examples, the tracks have been mixed with the chords on the left channel and the melody on the right channel. To practice playing chords beneath the melody, turn the balance knob on your stereo to the right (or remove your left headphone). To practice the melody using the audio for chord accompaniment only, turn the balance knob to the left. On most single-instrument examples, a metronome or "click track" is used to keep time. The click is often "panned" to the opposite side of the ukulele in the stereo field, so you may practice with as much or as little of the recorded ukulele as you need to help keep your place.

Contents

Tuning to the Audio

Now let's take a moment to check the tuning of your ukulele. In Level One, we learned the process of relative tuning and the options available, such as electronic tuners and pitch pipes, to assist in this necessary step.

Track 3 contains the correct pitch of each string beginning with the G string (fourth string), and continuing in order with the C string (third), E string (second), and A string (first). Carefully adjust the appropriate tuning peg while plucking the string to hear its pitch until it matches the reference pitch on the track.

When tuned correctly, the open strings of the ukulele play this little melody:

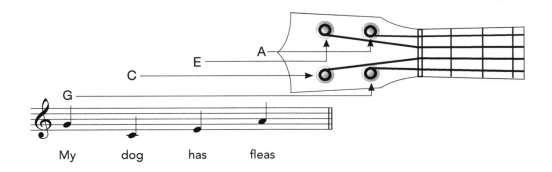

My   dog   has   fleas

Tuning Notes

The Fourth String:	G
The Third String:	C
The Second String:	E
The First String:	A

Ukulele History: The Jumping Flea

An instrument called the *braguinha* came to Hawaii with immigrants from the Portuguese island of Madiera in 1879. It is said that an immigrant, Joao Fernandes, began playing the braguinha on the pier upon his arrival. He dazzled the native Hawaiians with the sounds he coaxed from the little instrument with his facile playing. They thought his fingers resembled jumping fleas as they moved about the fingerboard. Thus, the braguinha became known as the "ukulele," which means "jumping flea" in Hawaiian.

Track 4

Lesson 1 | # Review of Level One

In *Play Ukulele Today! Level One*, you learned the parts of the ukulele, how to hold your ukulele, the fundamentals of reading music, how to play simple chords and melodies, general thumb and finger strumming, and the use of a felt pick. Major and minor scales were covered, as well as all the notes on the first three strings up to the fifth fret, encompassing first and second positions. Now, we shall take time to briefly review these notes and positions.

Review of First and Second Position

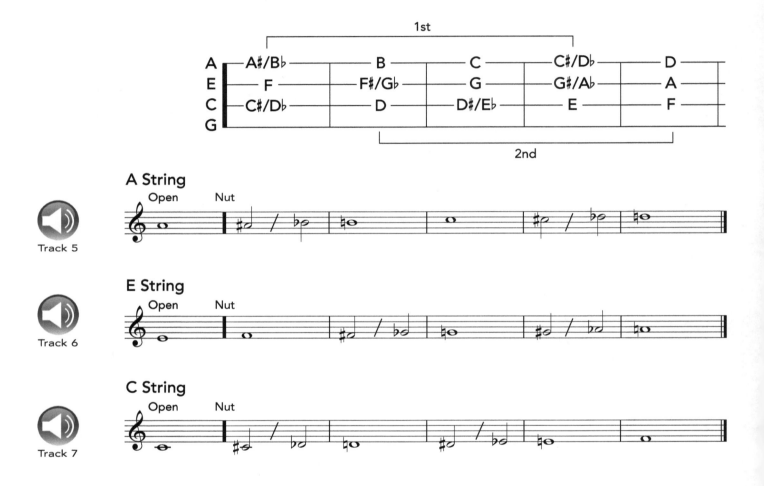

Track 5

Track 6

Track 7

Position Playing

Position playing is a system where your fingers cover the frets in succession. The position you're in is determined by the fret at which the first finger (index) is anchored. For example, in *first* position your index finger is located at the first fret, middle finger at the second fret, ring finger at the third fret, and pinky at the fourth fret.

Starting with first position, let's play a couple of chromatic exercises to cover all of these notes in order. Below is a chromatic scale, starting on C.

Chromatic Scale

A *chromatic scale* or 12-tone scale contains all twelve pitches of the Western scale. It's made up entirely of half steps, or semi-tones, and proceeds from one half step to the next. It could be considered the scale from which all others are derived.

Typically, sharped notes are used when ascending, and flatted notes are used when descending.

Chromatic Scale

Track 8

Ascending Chromatic Scale

Descending Chromatic Scale

This next exercise will cover all the notes and fingerings possible on the first three strings in first position.

First Down Flat

Track 9

Picking Melodies

When picking single note melody lines with your right (or picking) hand, you may choose from a few methods:

*   Downstrokes of the thumb – this provides a nice, strong tone. However, in faster tempos, this may become awkward.

*   Picking down with the thumb and up with the index finger – this works great for faster tunes and passages.

*   Pick alternating upstrokes with the first and second fingers – this method is used extensively by classical and flamenco guitarists.

*   Alternating downstrokes and upstrokes with the first finger or thumb, using it like a pick – this method is a bit unorthodox, but worthy of experimentation.

Now that we've reviewed the notes in first position, let's try a few tunes!

Track 10

Beautiful Dreamer

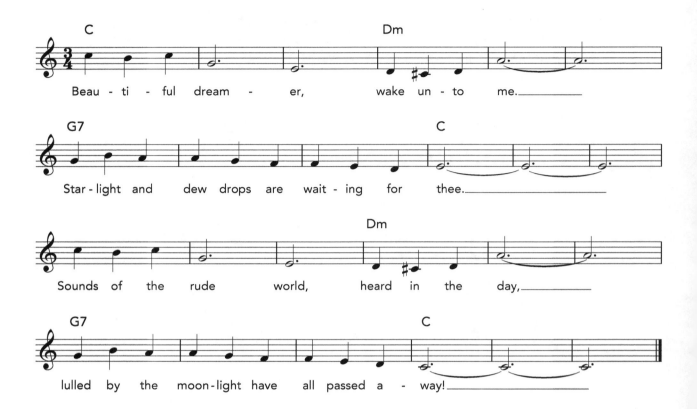

Beau - ti - ful dream - er, wake un - to me._____

Star - light and dew drops are wait - ing for thee._____

Sounds of the rude world, heard in the day,_____

lulled by the moon - light have all passed a - way!_____

Track 11

New Chord: Gm

Gm

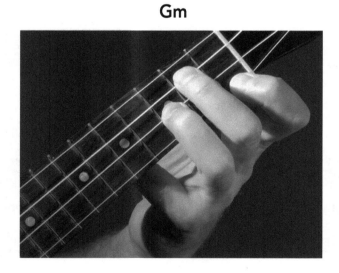

0 2 3 1

In addition to the new Gm chord, this beautiful piece provides a great review of first-position notes, as well as a revisiting of a variety of chords. The changes are frequent, so take it nice and easy with even quarter-note downstrokes of the thumb.

Track 12

O Come, O Come Immanuel

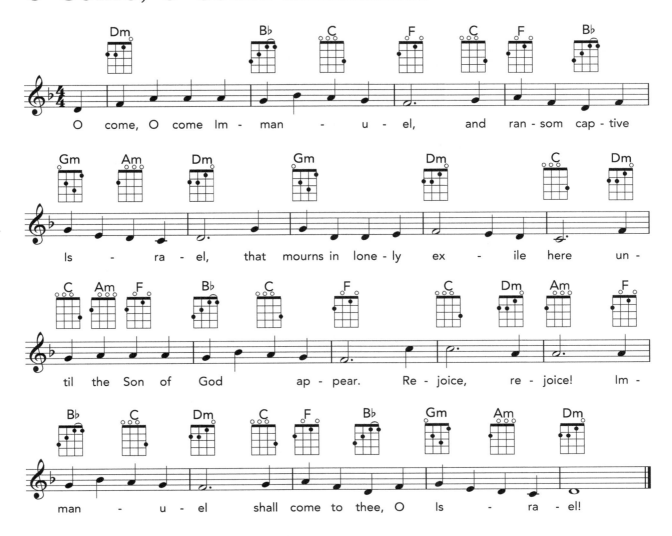

Now, let's take a look at second position. Remember to start with your first finger at the second fret.

Track 13

Spider Walk

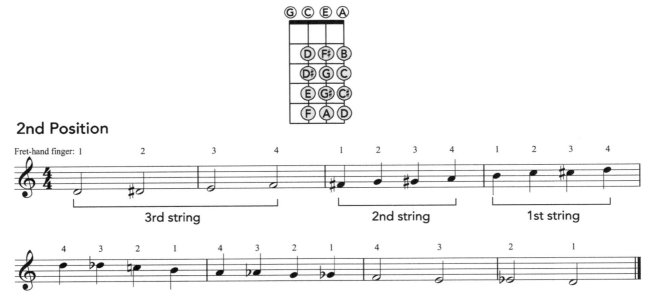

2nd Position

Here's a familiar melody that you may play entirely in the second position.

Itsy Bitsy Spider

▶ Remember to play the A note at fret 5 on the second string with your fourth finger.

If we add one note to the "Spider Walk" pattern at the first fret, first string (A♯ or B♭), we get a movable chromatic scale.

Movable Chromatic Scale

Movable
Chromatic Pattern

To play "In the Hall of the Mountain King," we'll start in first position, switch briefly to second position at the end of measures 3 and 7, and then return to first position to complete measures 4 and 8.

With regards to chords, this song has a couple we have not seen before: E and E♭. This is a closed chord form, which makes it movable, thus enabling it to be used for different chords as it's moved up the neck. From E, the E♭ is the same form, but one fret down.

Track 16

New Chords: E and E♭

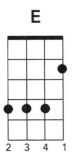

E

E♭

In this next song, your second and third fingers should maintain their placement on the 4th and 3rd strings as you move between the Dm, E, and E♭ chords.

Track 17

► Note that the open A string, just before and after the position shifts, gives us a smooth transfer point to make the shifts.

In the Hall of the Mountain King

Lesson 2 | Notes on the Fourth String: G

In Level One, we covered all the notes in both first and second position on the first, second, and third strings. This gives us a good understanding of how the notes progress on a linear level. For a more thorough knowledge of the instrument, we must also become familiar with the notes on the fourth string, G. This will not only help our chord playing, but also our melodic playing as we delve into fingerstyle.

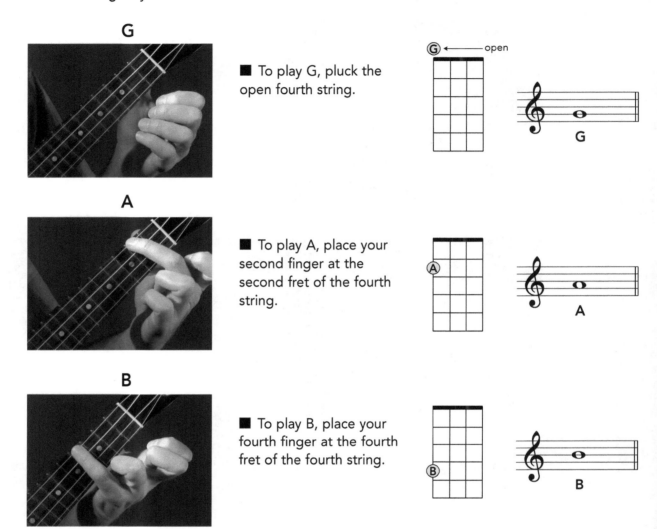

■ To play G, pluck the open fourth string.

■ To play A, place your second finger at the second fret of the fourth string.

■ To play B, place your fourth finger at the fourth fret of the fourth string.

These are notes we already know, but, as is the case with most of the notes on the instrument, they can be found in more than one place. G is the same note as fret 3 on string 2, and A is the same as our open first string.

Fourth String Study

Accidentals on the 4th String: G♯/A♭ and A♯/B♭

G♯/A♭

■ To play the note G♯ (or its enharmonic equivalent, A♭), place your first finger at the first fret of the fourth string.

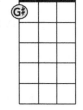 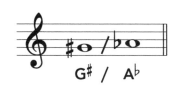

G♯ / A♭

A♯/B♭

■ To play the note A♯ (or its enharmonic equivalent, B♭), place your third finger at the third fret of the fourth string.

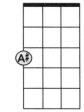 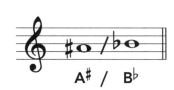

A♯ / B♭

Track 21

Happy Accidentals

Let's try some examples that include notes played on both the third and fourth strings.

Track 22

Ups & Downs

11

C & G String Boogie

3rd String   4th String

We have now covered all the notes in the first position on the fourth string. For us to round out our knowledge of first and second positions, there is one more fourth-string note to cover at the fifth fret: C. This is the same pitch as the C we know on the first string, third fret. Remember that, when in second position, your first finger is at the second fret, and each finger covers the notes in succession up to the fifth fret.

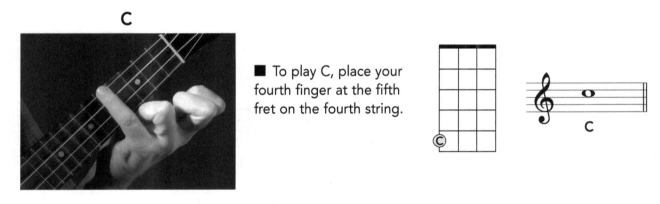

C

■ To play C, place your fourth finger at the fifth fret on the fourth string.

Try out the melody to "Go Tell Aunt Rhody" played entirely on the fourth string.

Go Tell Aunt Rhody (I've Got the Fourth String in My Head)

Common Stroke & Waltz Stroke

Track 26

The basic principle of strumming chords with the common stroke was covered in Level One. When playing in a quarter-note (or downbeat) rhythm, we use downstrokes (⊓) with the thumb.

For eighth-note rhythms, we strum down (⊓) with the thumb on the beat and up (V) with the index finger on the "and" or upbeats.

Continue to work on this concept and master it.

Another version of the common stroke would be the ***index finger strum***. For this stroke, arch your index finger about halfway between fully curled into your hand and completely extended. Curl your other fingers into your palm, and use the tip of your index finger, positioning it roughly above the twelfth fret. Strum with your index finger on both the upstrokes and downstrokes. This is somewhat similar to using a pick.

The ***waltz stroke***, or how we strum in 3/4 time, can be done by strumming down with the thumb once and up twice with the index finger. This covers the three quarter-note beats and helps get a lilting waltz feel, while also giving the strum a little finesse.

Here are some new chords: A7, E7, D, and D7. Let's try them in some common and waltz stroke exercises and songs. Play them using both thumb and finger combinations as well as the index finger strum.

Track 27

New Chords: A7, E7, D, and D7

A7

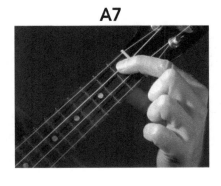

D

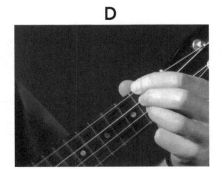

E7

D7

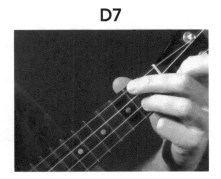

First and Second Endings

The following exercises have a *first and second ending*, indicated by brackets with the numbers 1 and 2. When you reach the repeat sign in the first ending (:‖), go back to the beginning. On the second time through, skip the first ending and go on to the second ending.

Track 28

Common Stroke 1

Track 29

Common Stroke 2

Track 30

Waltz Stroke

Play the chords to this next tune using the waltz stroke. You can also try picking out the melody.

Waltz Stroke Accompaniment

Track 31

My Bonnie Lies Over the Ocean

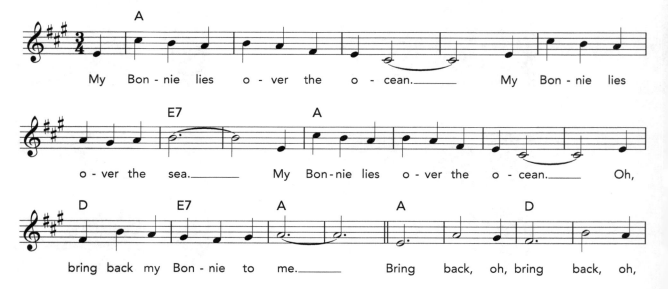

My Bon-nie lies o-ver the o-cean._____ My Bon-nie lies

o-ver the sea._____ My Bon-nie lies o-ver the o-cean._____ Oh,

bring back my Bon-nie to me._____ Bring back, oh, bring back, oh,

14

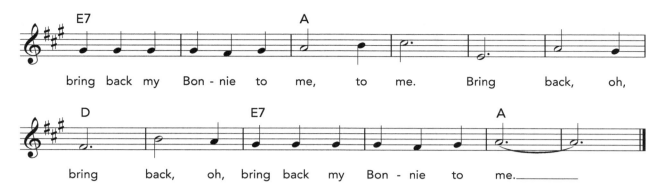

bring back my Bon - nie to me, to me. Bring back, oh,

bring back, oh, bring back my Bon - nie to me._____

Dotted Notes

As we know, a dot extends any note by one half its value.

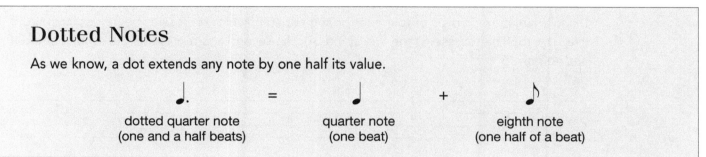

Strum this Hawaiian favorite using the given common stroke accompaniment, and then pick out the melody as well.

Common Stroke Accompaniment

Track 32

Aloha Oe

Ukulele History: Queen Liliuokalani

The last monarch of Hawaii was an avid musician and composer of over 150 songs, "Aloha Oe" being the most famous. She was a ukulele player and, like her brother, King Kalakauaua before her, did much to promote the popularity of the uke with the Hawaiian people. It was Queen Liliuokalani's claim that the name "ukulele" meant "the gift that came here," from the words "uku" (gift) and "lele" (to come).

Lesson 4 | Tablature

Up to this point, we've learned and utilized standard music notation to play our exercises and melodies. This is very helpful in understanding music as a whole and in referencing a multitude of musical literary sources that may not necessarily be specific to the ukulele. However, there is another form of musical notation called *tablature*. This is a system of musical notation that's specific to an instrument. It has been used for hundreds of years, and, in fact, a substantial amount of early lute and keyboard manuscript was written in tablature.

Ukulele tablature consists of four lines on the tab staff, which represent the four strings of the uke. The top line represents the first string (A), the second line represents the second string (E), and so on.

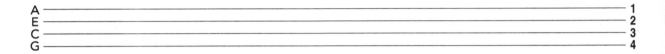

Tablature is essentially a road map of the fretboard and tells you exactly where to play a note as you travel through a tune.

Reading Pitches

Numbers are placed on the lines to indicate at which fret a note is to be played. The number "0" is used for open strings.

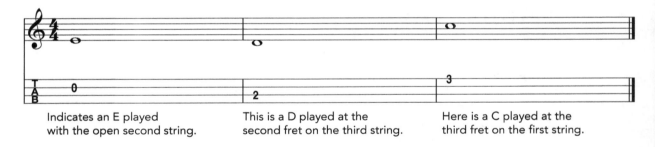

Indicates an E played with the open second string.

This is a D played at the second fret on the third string.

Here is a C played at the third fret on the first string.

Reading Rhythms

The tab staff is divided into measures, just like standard notation. When rhythm values are used in tab, they are indicated as follows. Rests and dotted note values appear as they do in standard notation.

whole note · half notes · quarter notes · eighth notes · dotted half note · quarter rest

Pushing Boundaries

Track 34

Review of Movable Scales

Toward the end of Level One, we learned about movable major and minor scales. Let's take a moment to review the patterns and look at how we may use these concepts to help move us up the neck. This will open the door to melodies and chordal possibilities that we cannot achieve in first and second positions alone. In addition, we'll gain a greater understanding of the ukulele.

Here are our movable major and minor scale patterns:

▶ Circled note = root note. These patterns may be moved to any root/position on the neck to play the desired scale.

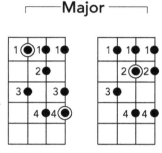

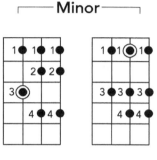

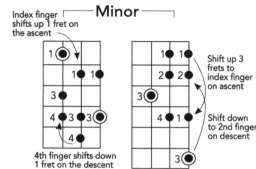

The first four of these scale patterns are in a box form, which means your fingers maintain one position. However, for us to play the complete minor scale (from root to its octave), we must shift positions within the patterns.

Let's apply these final patterns to an E minor scale to help illustrate how to make these shifts. This will bring us up to the fifth position. We've seen most of these notes, but in lower positions. Please refer to the tablature to familiarize yourself with their placement on the fingerboard in the higher positions. Before you play the scales, here are three notes in the fifth position we haven't seen thus far: high E♭, E, and F.

Track 35

E♭/D♯

■ To play E♭ (or its enharmonic equivalent, D♯), place your second finger at the sixth fret of the first string.

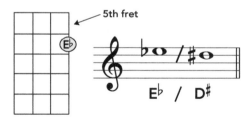

E

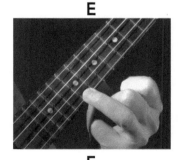

■ To play E in the fifth position, use your third finger at the seventh fret.

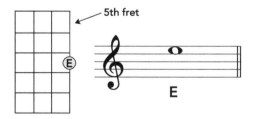

F

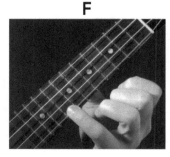

■ To play the F in the fifth position, put your fourth finger at the eighth fret.

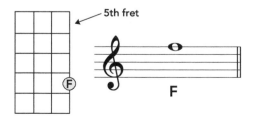

E Minor Scale 1

This pattern includes a shift between adjacent strings.

E Minor Scale 2

This pattern includes a shift on a single string.

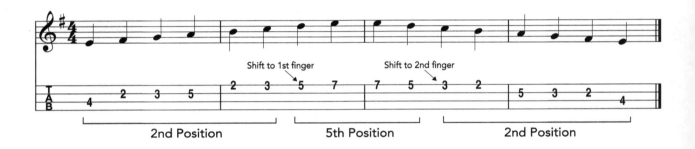

Now, let's put these concepts to use and play some tunes. Starting in the fifth position, we'll play a couple of holiday numbers, employing both major and minor keys.

"Joy to the World" is a popular Christmas melody that utilizes all the notes of the major scale. We'll be playing it in the key of F major, with the root on the third string at the fifth fret.

 Track 37

Joy to the World

Next, we'll play "We Three Kings of Orient Are." This piece starts in G minor, with the root on the third string at the seventh fret. It concludes in B♭ major, with the root on the second string at the sixth fret.

Track 38

We Three Kings of Orient Are

Now, let's go to the seventh position to try a couple of classic traditional melodies: "Shady Grove" and "Miss MacLeod's Reel," in A minor and G major, respectively. We have two unfamiliar notes in this position: F♯ and G.

Track 39

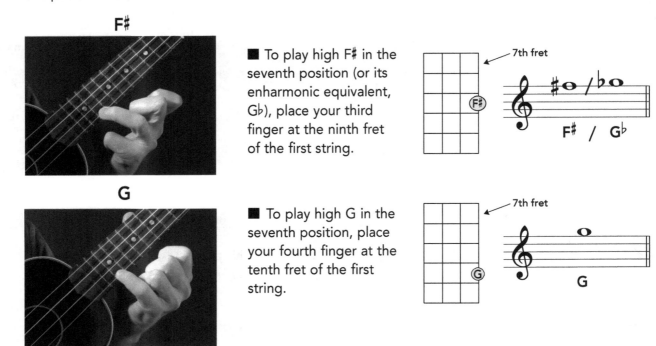

■ To play high F♯ in the seventh position (or its enharmonic equivalent, G♭), place your third finger at the ninth fret of the first string.

■ To play high G in the seventh position, place your fourth finger at the tenth fret of the first string.

As previously mentioned, use the tablature to help familiarize yourself with the new locations of notes in this higher position.

After you learn the melody, strum the chords and sing along.

Shady Grove

Track 40

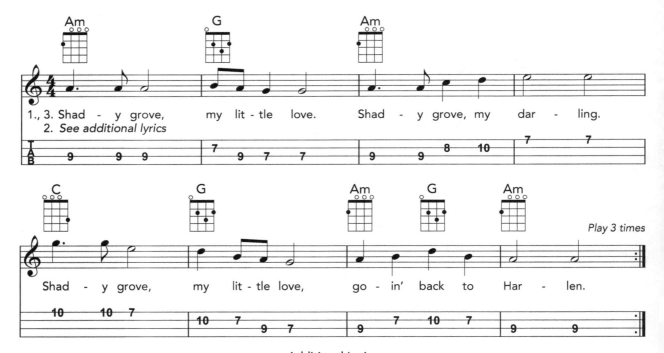

1., 3. Shad - y grove, my lit - tle love. Shad - y grove, my dar - ling.
2. See additional lyrics

Shad - y grove, my lit - tle love, go - in' back to Har - len.

Play 3 times

Additional Lyrics

2. Peaches in the summertime,
   Apples in the fall.
   If I don't find the gal I love,
   I don't want none at all.

Miss MacLeod's Reel

This next piece requires a momentary shift from the seventh to the tenth position (to reach the high A). Also, we have some new notes: G#/A♭ and high A.

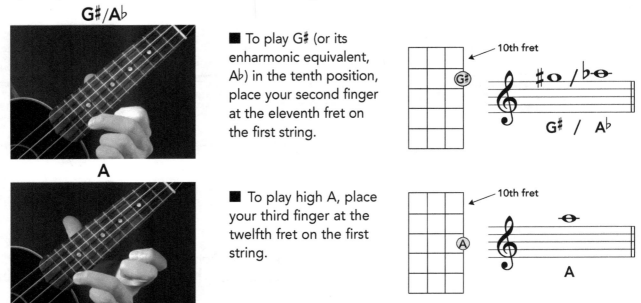

- To play G# (or its enharmonic equivalent, A♭) in the tenth position, place your second finger at the eleventh fret on the first string.

- To play high A, place your third finger at the twelfth fret on the first string.

Track 43

God Rest Ye Merry, Gentlemen

God rest ye mer-ry, gen-tle-men, let noth-ing you dis - may. For Je - sus Christ our

Sav - ior was born up-on this day, to save us all from Sa - tan's pow'r when

we were gone a - stray. O___ tid - ings of com - fort and joy, com-fort and

joy. O___ tid - ings of com - fort and joy!___

Now you should know all the notes up to the twelfth fret, in one position or another. Keep in mind that position playing is a valuable tool at your disposal—not a rule that can't be broken. You should feel free to arrange and play melodies in whatever way works best for you.

Movable Chord Shapes

Track 44

The easiest and most efficient way to expand our chord vocabulary is through the use of *movable chord shapes*. A movable chord shape is simply a chord with no open strings. These shapes can be used anywhere on the neck, giving you as many as a dozen different chords. All of these shapes stem from our open chords, but our fingerings usually require some repositioning to accommodate the first finger barring over, or at least covering, any fret that would have been previously open.

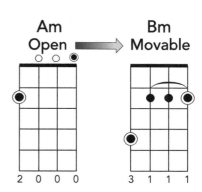

◉ = root

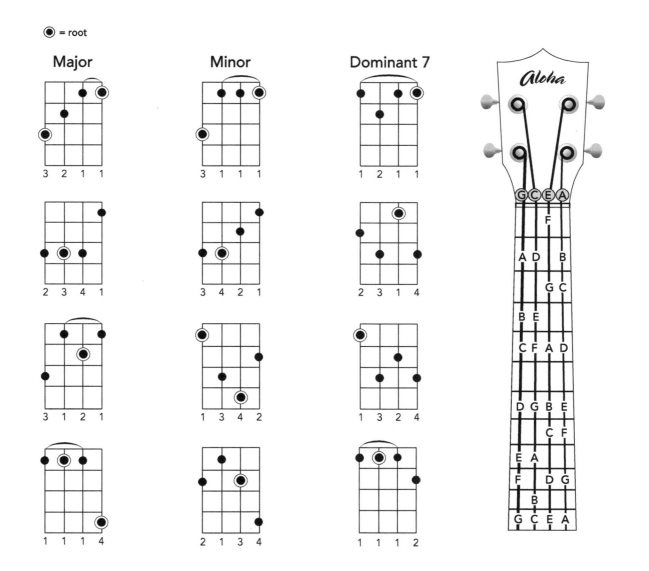

Hammer-Ons, Pull-Offs & Slides

Hammer-ons, pull-offs, and *slides* are invaluable left-hand techniques. When employed, you cause two or more notes to sound by only picking the string once.

Hammer-Ons

To execute a *hammer-on*, you pick the first note (open or fretted) and then decisively (but rhythmically in time) bring the tip of the appropriate finger down at the fret of the second (higher) note on the same string. When sufficient force is used, this causes the second note to sound without having to be picked.

> The hammer-on is indicated by a *slur* from a lower note to a higher note. The *slur* is a curved line in music that looks identical to a tie, except it connects different pitches together, indicating a *legato* feel. *Legato* is a musical term that means smooth and connected, without breaks between the successive tones.

Hammer-On from an Open String

Hammer-On from a Fretted Note

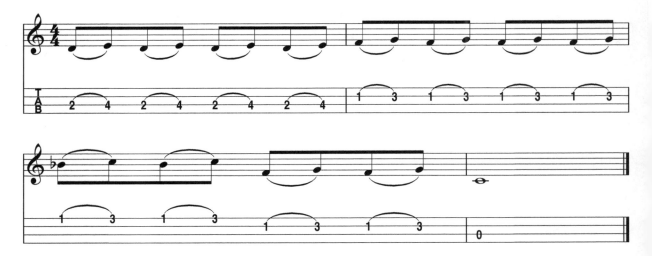

24

Pull-Offs

Track 48

In order to perform a *pull-off*, sound the fretted higher note with your picking hand, then pull off the finger fretting that note in a slightly downward motion, so it actually plucks (and sounds) the fretted or open lower note below it.

The pull-off is indicated by a slur from a higher note to a lower one.

Track 49

Pull-Off to an Open String

Track 50

Pull-Off to a Fretted Note

Track 51

She'll Be Comin' 'Round the Mountain

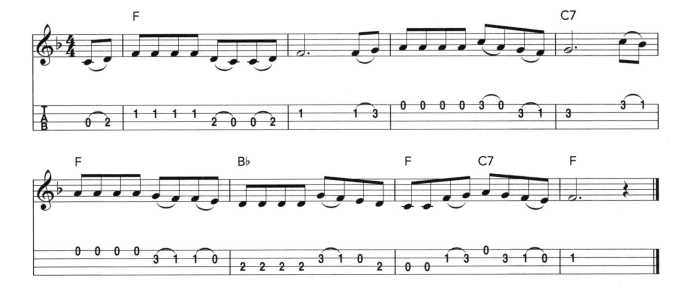

Play the melody of this next tune that features hammer-ons and pull-offs. When playing the chords for this song, try out some of our movable forms in the second section.

Track 52

Jack of Diamonds

Slides

To execute a *slide*, you pick a fretted note and, while maintaining pressure, move (or slide) your finger up or down the fretboard to the desired second note.

> The slide is indicated by a straight line positioned at an upward or downward angle between two notes.

The second note, or destination note, can be picked or not picked. If the second note is not to be picked, a slur also connects the two notes. Sometimes slides are used as embellishments, not necessarily tying two notes together. In this case, you begin the slide at an arbitrary point (usually lower), with no real rhythmic or tonal value, and then slide into the target pitch. These types of slides are notated with a sloped line before or after a single pitch.

Track 54

Slide Up

Track 55

Slide Up, Down & Around

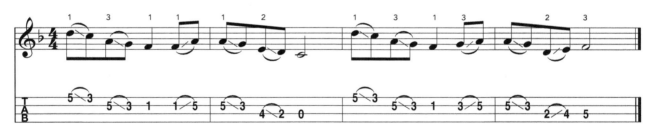

Track 56

Sourwood Mountain

Lesson 8 | Time Marches On

Track 57

Up to this point, we've played songs in both 4/4 (common time) and 3/4 (waltz time). These meters are part of a group called *simple time signatures*. There are a good many other ways that a beat can be laid down for a tune. We'll now explore a couple of these other meters.

Cut Time

Cut time, usually indicated on the staff by (¢), is 2/2 time signature. This means there are two beats per measure, and the half note gets the beat. This meter, also known as "alla breve," has an accelerated and driving feel and is a common time signature for marches.

> *Alla breve* is Italian for "Alla" (according to the) + "Breve" (twice as fast as normal).

A New Road Map

D.S. al Fine, or *dal segno al fine*, literally means "[play] from the sign to the end." This is an indication to start back at the *segno* (𝄋) and continue playing until you reach the word "fine."

D.C. al Fine, or *da capo al fine*, means "from the head [beginning] to the end." This is an indication to repeat back to the beginning of the music and continue until you reach the word "fine."

Let's try playing this familiar march to get the feel of cut time. To play an accompaniment strum, two solid downstrokes work well for a downbeat emphasis.

Cut Time Accompaniment

Marine's Hymn

Track 58

Introducing 16th Notes

If you divide an eighth note in half, you get a sixteenth note. A sixteenth note looks like an eighth note, but it has two flags on its stem instead of one:

Consecutive sixteenth notes are connected with a double beam:

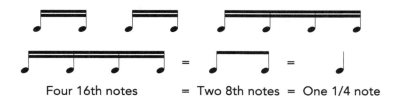

If we count the quarter note beat while tapping our foot and eighth notes by putting "and" between the beats, we can count sixteenth notes by adding the syllables "e" and "a" between the eighth notes: "1-e-and-a."

A sixteenth rest is counted in the same manner.

2/4 Time

Sixteenth notes are a common rhythmic figure in 2/4 time. In 2/4 time, the quarter note gets the beat, and there are two beats per measure. This time signature is commonly used for polkas, fiddle tunes, and many other traditional or folk melodies.

Unlike 2/2, where a very straight ahead downbeat approach works well, 2/4 either accents the second beat and/or the "and" of both beats. Here's an example.

Now we come to another stroke that can be very effective in 2/4 time...

The Pick Stroke

With the *pick stroke*, we pick a single note with our thumb on the downbeat (usually on strings three or four) and strum up with the index finger on the upbeat, or the "and."

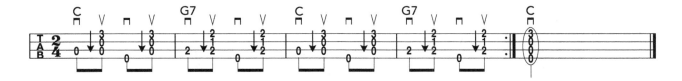

Time to get out the dancin' shoes and play a 2/4 tune! The melody is written on the top staff and the accompaniment chord pattern is shown on the tablature staff below. Be sure to try out both parts.

Track 60

► Keep thumb alternating between the third and fourth strings throughout.

Oh, Them Golden Slippers

Time & Time Again

Track 61

Compound Time

Compound time signatures have a beat that is subdivided by three. Some typical compound time signatures are 6/8, 9/8, and 12/8. For example, 6/8 time indicates that we count six eighth notes per measure, or two groups of three.

Triplets

Triplets are units of three eighth notes played in the space of one beat. In compound time signatures, the foot taps in the space of a dotted quarter note. We subdivide those dotted quarter notes into three eighth notes, counted with emphasis on the first note of the set: **1**-2-3, **2**-2-3, etc. You may also get the proper rhythm by saying "tri-puh-let, tri-puh-let," or "1-and-uh, 2-and-uh," etc.

Triplets also occur in simple time signatures, though not as frequently, and may be counted in much the same way. In 4/4, start with the quarter-note beat, counting 1, 2, 3, 4:

Then divide that into even eighth-note divisions: 1 & 2 & 3 & 4 &:

Now, if we squeeze an extra eighth note evenly into the same space as these two, we get a triplet: **1** 2 3, **2** 2 3, **3** 2 3, **4** 2 3:

Triplets in simple time signatures are always notated with a "3" at the beam to indicate there are three notes in the space of two.

Play the familiar melody below in 6/8 time, then strum the chords using this accompaniment pattern:

6/8 Time Accompaniment

Track 62

Hickory Dickory Dock

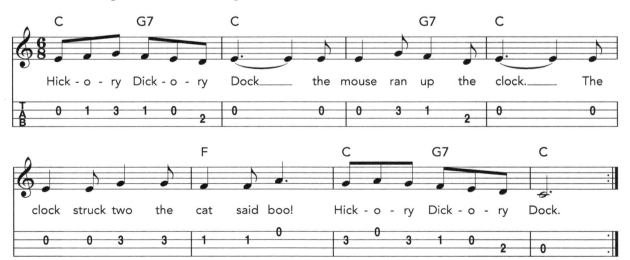

31

Triplet Stroke

To strum a *triplet stroke*, we:

1. Strum down (⊓) with the index finger.

2. Follow with a downstroke (⊓) of the thumb.

3. Then, strum up (∨) with the index finger.

To get the feel of this and other strokes, it can be helpful to mute the strings with your fret hand to create a percussive (drum beat) sound while you strum. Just lightly touch the strings with your fret hand without pushing them down to the fretboard. This method enables you to hear the accuracy of your rhythms a little more clearly. You can also use this technique to occasionally add a rhythmic spice to your playing.

Triplet Exercise 1

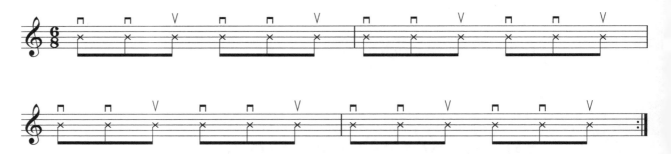

Sometimes the syllables of words can help you learn a rhythm.

Triplet Exercise 2

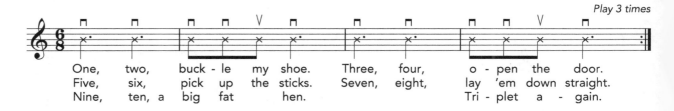

Play 3 times

One, two, buck - le my shoe. Three, four, o - pen the door.
Five, six, pick up the sticks. Seven, eight, lay 'em down straight.
Nine, ten, a big fat hen. Tri - plet a - gain.

Now here's a fun triplet tune in 4/4 time that includes the triplet stroke and the muted-string technique.

Track 66

Triplet Your Uke
(When You're Happy and You Know It)

Track 67

New Chords: F7 and B♭m

(From our movable-form arsenal)

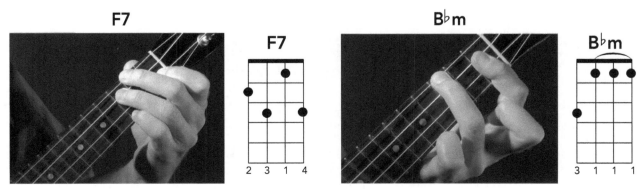

33

Here, we'll strum triplets in 12/8 time, which is often referred to as "doo wop" time. It's used for many songs from the '50s, as well as slow blues.

Track 68

Da Uke Doo Wop

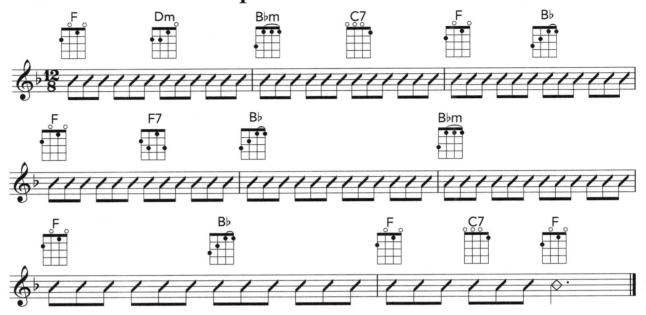

First play the chords with a triplet stroke, then pluck the melody to this timeless classic.

Triplet Stroke Accompaniment

Track 69

When Johnny Comes Marching Home

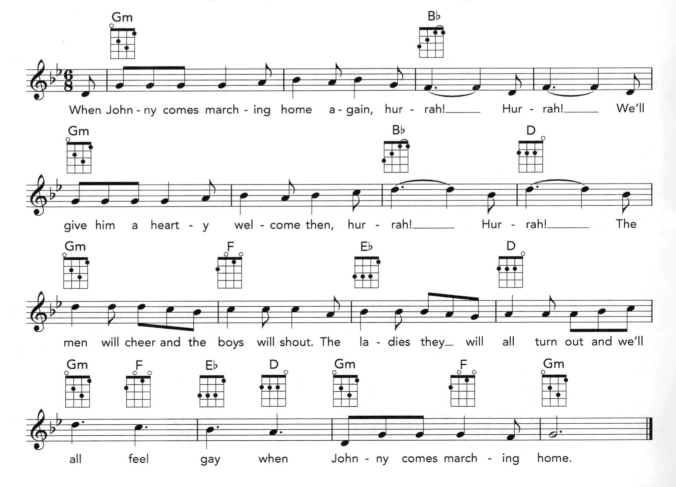

The Shuffle Stroke

The **shuffle stroke** is similar to the common stroke, generally used in 4/4 time, and associated with boogie-woogie blues and jazz. It also works well in compound and other meters. You've already heard an example of the shuffle used on the song "Triplet Your Uke" on page 33. Eighth notes are played unevenly or "swung"—the first note played long and the second note short. This is timed as if you were playing a triplet with the first two notes tied together:

The pulse is also accented more heavily on the second and fourth beats, as opposed to the first and third. There is an extra dash of spice, which can be thrown into a shuffle to really add some "boogie" to its "woogie," by switching on and off between a chord tone and an additional note (usually a whole step above) on every other beat. This creates a pendulum-like, rocking back-and-forth feel. This "boogie beat" concept was put into play by early barrelhouse pianists and has been carried on through blues and rock and roll.

Shuffle Boogie

► In this case, we add a D note on the third string to both chords every second and fourth beat.

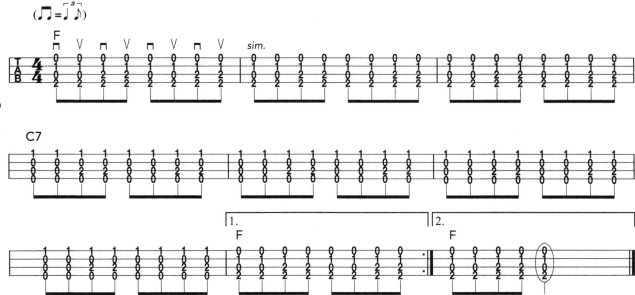

This handy progression could be used to fit many songs, such as "Polly Wolly Doodle," "Iko, Iko," and the ukulele classic, "It Ain't Gonna Rain No Mo'."

Ukulele History: Wendell Hall

Known as the "red-headed music maker," Wendell Hall was an early star of the ukulele on the vaudeville stage, radio, and on record. His 1923 recording of "It Ain't Gonna Rain No Mo'" was a multi-million seller and spent six weeks at number one on the U.S. charts.

New Chords: C6 and D♭6

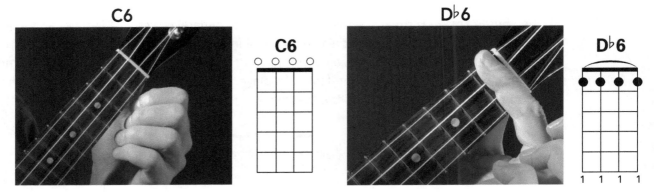

In this classic blues song, we'll demonstrate how effective it can be to vary the rhythms by switching up our strokes. Centering on a shuffle, adding triplets and straight quarter-note downstrokes at key points gives this 12-bar blues the depth it deserves.

See See Rider

Additional Lyrics

2. I'm goin' away, baby, won't be back till fall.
   Goin' away, baby, won't be back till fall.
   If I find a good gal, I won't be back at all.

Lesson 10 | Fingerpicking

Track 74

Fingerpicking on the ukulele can encompass essentially all melodic and harmonic playing that is approached without the use of a pick. Historically, most ukulele playing has been done with the fingerstyle technique.

Picking with the fingers offers a great many options for voicings and textures on the ukulele—things that would be difficult, if not impossible, with the sole use of the pick. Let's take a look at some specifics.

As we learned in Level One, the fingers on the fret hand are numbered from index to pinky: 1, 2, 3, and 4. The fingers on the picking hand have their own designations. These letters are abbreviations from the internationally known system of Spanish words and letters:

p	pulgar	=	thumb
i	indice	=	index finger
m	medio	=	middle finger
a	anular	=	ring finger

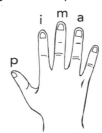

Arpeggios

Arpeggios, or broken chords, are a huge part of fingerpicking, both for song accompaniment and for instrumental solos. This means that we play the notes in a chord individually (often in succession), as opposed to strumming, where they are played all at once. There are many different picking patterns and combinations available, so experiment with as many as you can discover.

Let's try a few arpeggios...

Arpeggio 1

Track 75

Arpeggio 2

Track 76

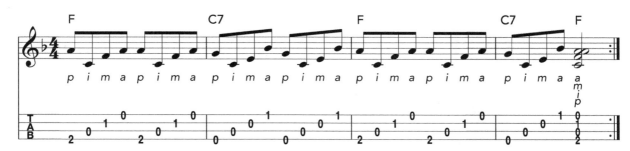

Alternate Thumb 1

► Keep your thumb switching between the third and fourth strings.

Alternate Thumb 2

P.M. Lullaby

Picking Blues

Here's a classic fingerpicking tune in 6/8 time.

House of the Rising Sun

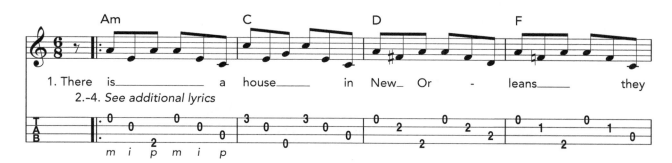

1. There is_____ a house_____ in New__ Or - leans_____ they
2.-4. *See additional lyrics*

m i p m i p

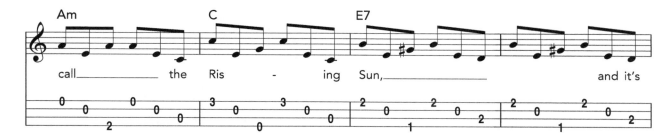

call_____ the Ris - ing Sun,_____ and it's

been_____ the ruin_____ of man - y a poor boy, and

God,_____ I know_____ I'm one. _____

Additional Lyrics

2. If I had listened to what mama said,
   I'd 'a' been at home today.
   Being so young and foolish, poor girl,
   Let a gambler lead me astray.

3. My mother, she's a tailor,
   She sews my new blue jeans.
   My sweetheart's a drunkard, Lord,
   Drinks down in New Orleans.

4. The only thing a drunkard needs
   Is a suitcase and a trunk.
   The only time he's ever satisfied
   Is when he's on a drunk.

Playing Two Parts at Once

We have now learned many different types of melodies and a variety of ways in which we may accompany them with chords. Now, let's take a look at some new ways to fill out our playing by adding harmonies to melodies and melodic elements to chords.

Parallel 3rds & 6ths

One very effective way to harmonize a melody is with the use of *parallel 3rds* and/or *6ths*. For example, if we take a melody note and stack a *3rd* on top of it, we create a harmony, or two parts played simultaneously.

What do we mean by *3rds*? Well, we need to look at a major scale to find the answer. Here is a C major scale (but any scale can work). If we number each note of the scale 1–8:

...with C, the root, being "1," then E would fall on "3," which makes it the 3rd. Play these two notes together, and we have the harmony of a 3rd.

3rd

We can continue this all the way up the scale, effectively harmonizing each note with the successive 3rd above. A 3rd above D is F, a 3rd above E is G, and so on. Visually, this can be observed in the written music by "stacking" the note in the next space or the next line. Some 3rds are major (two whole steps apart), some are minor (a whole and a half step apart):

Major 3rd   Minor 3rd   Minor 3rd

Basic chords (or *triads*) are constructed by stacking a 3rd on top of a 3rd.

C major   D minor
chord   chord

Now, it's time to play through a few scale combinations, harmonizing with parallel 3rds. Pick these notes with individual fingers, or by "pinching" between the thumb and a finger.

Here's a C major scale harmonized in 3rds on the second and third strings.

C Major – Parallel 3rds

Here we have an F major scale harmonized in 3rds on the first and second strings.

F Major – Parallel 3rds

If we reverse the order of these note pairings—let's say C and E—with C being the higher of the two, then it becomes a 6th, because E is six notes below C. The sound of 6ths is used in many types of music, from Hawaiian to blues and swing, just to name a few.

Here are some scale exercises demonstrating parallel 6ths.

C Major – Parallel 6ths

A Major – Parallel 6ths

Now check out this Hawaiian waltz featuring both parallel 3rds and 6ths.

Isle of My Love

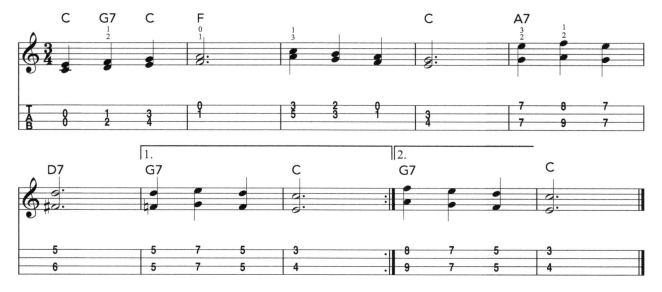

The Dotted Eighth Note

The next tune includes this new rhythm, the *dotted eighth note*.

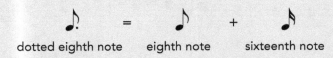

dotted eighth note   eighth note   sixteenth note

Dotted eighth notes are sometimes beamed together with sixteenth notes to create this rhythm:

Track 88

Battle Hymn of the Republic

Mine eyes have seen the glo-ry of the com-ing of the Lord; He is tramp-ling out the vin-tage where the grapes of wrath are stored. He hath loosed the fate-ful light-ning of His ter-ri-ble swift sword, His truth is march-ing on. Glo-ry, glo-ry hal-le-lu-jah! Glo-ry, glo-ry hal-le-lu-jah! Glo-ry, glo-ry hal-le-lu-jah! His truth is march-ing on.

The first part of this piece incorporates a "pinch" between the thumb and middle finger on the fourth and second strings, alternating with the index finger playing the upbeats on the third string. The second part has the index and middle playing together on the downbeat, while the thumb plays the upbeat.

Track 89

Andantino

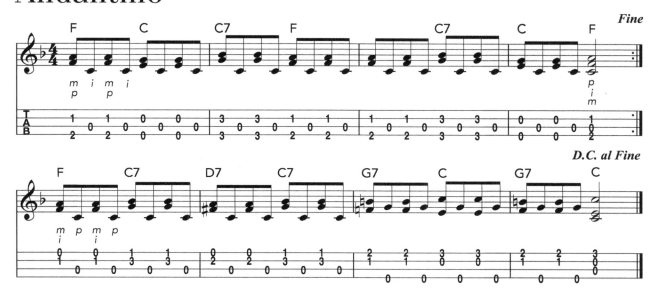

Chord Melody

In the following arrangements, we use a **sweep stroke**. To accomplish this, we sweep down through a chord with the thumb until we arrive at the desired melody note and give it a little more emphasis. Employing this technique as we pick through a melody enables us to play both chords and melodies simultaneously.

Track 90

Skip to My Lou

Track 91

Bingo

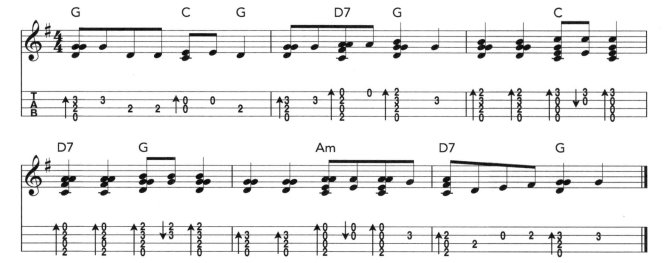

New Chords: E6, A6, and D6

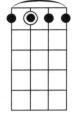

This is an easy, movable chord form for which we barre straight across all four strings.

The root note is found on the third string, so D6 is a full barre at the second fret, E6 is at the fourth fret, and A6 is at the ninth fret. This is the same form we've encountered previously as a D♭6.

Here are two more tunes arranged for chord-melody uke. "Corrina" includes the new barre chords as well as the "pinch" technique. The strum arrows in the tablature staff tell you where to use the sweep stroke to emphasize the melody notes.

Corrina

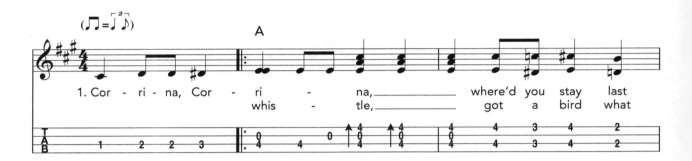

Danny Boy

Tremolo & the Roll Stroke

Tremolo

Given that notes on the ukulele quickly fade away after being picked, we must address how to create long, sustained tones, similar to that produced by wind and bowed instruments. For this to be achieved, we must use a technique called *tremolo*.

To play the tremolo stroke:

- Fold the second, third, and fourth fingers of your picking hand into your palm.

- For a focused tremolo, encompassing one or two strings, use only your index finger in rapid downstrokes and upstrokes. This movement stems largely from the main and second knuckles of the index finger, akin to a scratching motion.

- For a wider tremolo (strumming three to four strings), more wrist movement is required. Use of the nail yields a louder, more percussive sound.

This should be as quick and constant as possible, creating a flickering, beautiful shimmering effect. The next tune features this new technique (shown in the notation with slash marks:), as well as the new Fm chord.

New Chord: Fm

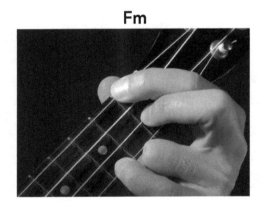

Cielito Lindo (My Pretty Darling)

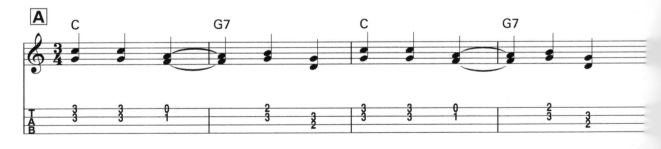

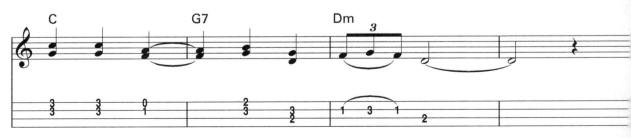

Track 97

The Roll Stroke

To play the (five finger) *roll stroke*, begin with your fingers curled into the palm of your picking hand. Fan your fingers out one by one across all of the strings in a continuous downward motion. Start with the pinky (fourth) finger, followed by the ring, middle, index fingers, and finish with the thumb, completing the roll stroke.

This next song, "Habenera" (from Bizet's *Carmen*), is a very cool Spanish-flavored piece. It works great to accompany this with all quarter-note downstrokes, adding the roll stroke on the third beat of every measure.

There's also a new, easy chord for this song: G6.

New Chord: G6

G6

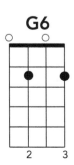

First play through the melody of this next tune, then try out the chord accompaniment with the roll stroke.

Roll Stroke Accompaniment

Habenera

48